Mushroom

foraging &
feasting

Victoria Romanoff

Mushroom

foraging & feasting

RECOLLECTIONS
AND RECIPES
FROM A LIFETIME
ON THE HUNT

Photography by Sarah Adams

ABBEVILLE PRESS PUBLISHERS
NEW YORK · LONDON

Contents

◦•◦

N.B. Most of these mushrooms flourish widely, but the growing seasons specified herein are for the northeastern U.S.

Introduction

World War II was already raging on the eastern front. Our tranquil life on the shores of the Baltic Sea was going to cease forever, but not before I found my very first mushroom. I was four years old and had wandered off to explore some large pine trees near our summer dacha, escorted only by my mother's loyal German shepherd, Willie. Poking through a dense needle blanket, I spotted a large mushroom with a light brown cap under the pines. The top felt greasy; the stem, sturdy and white, veiled in a pretty skirt. I brought this treasure to our cook, who proclaimed it to be edible, even choice. *Butterpilz* was its name! For supper that night, on our pine-scented veranda, it was served thin-sliced and sautéed, in a bowl of clear broth. I was bursting with pride. A very distant memory, that Baltic summer, but definitely my initiation to foraging. A passion that will last

The author with
chanterelles and cat

my entire life, I hope, and which was further refined by living in Displaced Persons camps during the lean last year of the war and those that followed, when hunting and gathering was no longer just an enjoyable pastime but a necessity for survival.

My next destination, the severely bombed and still hot German port of Hamburg, provided no grounds for mycological advances. A few months later, though, my mother and I found shelter in a D.P. barrack near a small village south of the big seaport. When September arrived, my mother, Tatiana, escorted me on my first serious wild mushroom hunt. A lifelong passion was born! Tatiana, born in Saint Petersburg and raised in Helsinki after the revolution, was completely obsessed with *po gribi* (a Russian idiomatic expression meaning "for the mushrooms"). The Nabokovs were friends and neighbors of my grandparents (who lived on Nevski Prospect) and many fall evenings were spent together sharing the day's bounty. The preparation deviated little: lots of butter, much sour cream, fresh dill, and porcini, accompanied by glasses of chilled champagne. Tatiana was a skilled instructor, introducing me to many basic edible species, as well as the evil ones. She felt strongly that if one knew the most poisonous ones thoroughly, there would be no risk of misidentification. What a joy it was to enter the magical, colorful, and mystical underworld of the fungus. Where else could one encounter dead man's fingers, jelly teeth, devil's tobacco, stinkhorns, slippery lizard tufts, scarlet elf cups, or the old man of the woods? Only in the deep forest, of course! We focused mostly on the *Boletus edulis*, the coroneted king of the huge mushroom clan. This robust species was big, handsome, prolific, and utterly delicious!

Competition was fierce. Entering the dark and balsamy woods at dawn, we saw several Polish women already emerging with baskets on their heads filled with this most desirable edible. Nevertheless, we succeeded. Tatiana would scan the thickly pine-needled floors and mossy blankets with a calm eye, and I would crawl under the prickly branches where only rodents could maneuver with ease. Thin and small at the age of six, I performed well. She spotted young button boletes, just rising from their cushy beds. Their caps were the palest sand color, and the stems white like a hard-boiled egg, with a lacy pattern of light gray lines. I found long specimens reaching for light next to the pine trunks.

Several hours later we had filled our baskets. We sat down in a small clearing; exhausted, scratched, and content, we cleaned our bounty with gentle brushing and minimal cutting. Just before we left the woods, Tatiana put some branches over our containers. "No need to advertise to the hungry world," she explained. This instilled in me the need to make a

The author and her mother, Tatiana, in their D.P. days, having just emerged from the woods with a bag of mushrooms. Both wear pants made by Tatiana from U.S. Army blankets.

mushroom hunt a quiet as well as a purposeful affair. One could share the bounty later, but it was best not to disclose prime locations.

How Tatiana procured butter to accompany the boletes in the fall of 1944 is still a mystery to me. In our camp there was no cooking oil, lard, or bacon. Some people fried frostbitten cull potatoes in candle paraffin, claiming that if the potatoes were eaten hot enough, one couldn't detect the awful-tasting, crust-forming wax. Perhaps she traded a piece of jewelry, her Leica camera, or a flask of Chanel No. 5, but she did return from a neighboring German farm with a large pat of butter, first wrapped in blue tissue paper and then rolled in several sheets of newsprint tied with string. We melted the luxurious substance in a frying pan on top of our small iron stove, from which rose a convoluted flue pipe, circling the ceiling prior to piercing the roof. All the prime specimens were thickly sliced and submerged in the bubbling butter. Older boletes and stems were thinly shaved, pierced with string, and wired just below the stovepipe for slow drying.

The aroma of the gently simmering boletes permeated our tiny room and escaped under the wool army blanket that served as our door. Supper was a triumph! A plate mounted with gold mushroom slices drizzled with brown butter and a handful of chopped wild herbs. Accompanying this was the usual slice of commissary bread, eaten carefully because these square and heavy loaves often contained pieces of bark and occasionally even shards of brick. My digestive system was not used to butter, but even a long time in the outhouse did not diminish the memory of this divine repast. Our neighbors received small samples on a scrap of the blue tissue. Sharing was one way of fortifying our diet, which for the most part was an uninterrupted monotony of rutabagas, frozen blackish cull potatoes, as well as the weekly allotment of commissary bread.

Mushrooms were picked into late October, before a bitter cold winter shut down mycological expeditions. In November we visited the woods to forage for dry branches, pinecones, and clumps of moss, anything that would burn in our voracious stove. The D.P. camp sat in a thick, sour haze all winter, fuel shortages the centerpiece of our cold lives. Mushroom hunting was replaced by coal procurement; this was accomplished by the smallest and most nimble camp inmates, like myself. Scrambling up on the trains at a nearby bend where the wagons slowed down, we kicked and scraped off as much coal as we could before the black iron cars accelerated again. Less athletic family members would then scurry to gather the black jewels glowing between the icy crushed stones of the track bed.

The author and her partner Sarah Adams with morels, circa 1977

The much yearned-for spring finally arrived, providing us with edible nettles. They had to be gathered with great skill and respect; full of needle-like fur, they could sting and burn for hours. However, steamed in salt water, nettles rendered tender, sweet, vitamin-rich greens, more interesting than spinach. I also learned to gather sour grass, wild garlic and onions, nuts, fruits, and a large variety of leaves and berries used for steeping medicinal tinctures and teas as well as other healing potions and salves.

By the time I emigrated to the United States as a teenager in the early 1950s, I had become a keen forager of flora, fauna, and fungi. These talents, though, were laid idle for the next decade. For several years, Tatiana and I were confined in urban centers like New York City (imagine picking mushrooms on Fifth Avenue), Syracuse, Providence, and Boston.

Mushroom picking and consuming became a major activity again in the mid-1960s, when I moved to upstate New York. The deep, mixed woods, farm fields, and cemeteries were blessed with every conceivable fungal fruiting. July of 1968 was record setting—it rained almost every day. Tiptoeing into the beech forest, one of my better hunting locations, I was overwhelmed with joy! The entire forest floor was bursting with bright yellow eruptions of chanterelles. Every few feet, in every direction, sat clusters of these delicious and socially compatible mushrooms. Racing back to the barn, I grabbed every bucket, laundry basket, cardboard box, and empty bag I could find and sped back to the woods. Several hours later, I had filled my truck with aromatic golden cargo.

My partner, who had some notion of how I might return, had cleared two long folding tables and set out tubs of water, brushes, and knives (all the paraphernalia needed to deal with the bounty). I invited friends and neighbors, promising an exquisite dinner after this cleaning and trimming marathon. We skewered baby chanterelles with pearl onions and cherry tomatoes, basted them with garlic oil, and roasted the kebabs on oak charcoal. This crunchy appetizer was followed with a thin-sliced chanterelle pizza embellished with lemon thyme and shaved parmesan. The next course was fresh cavatelli with a chopped chanterelle sauce, enriched with butter, cream, sweet vermouth, sun-dried tomato puree, and fresh basil. For the main course, I sectioned large chanterelles into long strips, which I sea salted and pan fried, garnished with chopped rosemary, and served with browned local pork sausages. We skipped dessert!

The following morning I implored my well-fed friends to help me with the remaining mountain of gold. We sat around long tables and worked late into the afternoon. By evening, we had tiny 'shrooms packed in oil and salt, teens in spicy vinegar, young adults in freezer bags cooling on ice, and mature ones sliced for drying.

After the banquet and the prolific preserving, I still had more than half of my bounty left. That night, I painted a poster depicting a handsome chanterelle taking a bow and listing its qualities, such as "looks good, great flavor, caloric modesty (when not simmered in butter and cream) and an affordable price at $7 per pound." The next morning, I drove to our local farmer's market with the poster, chanterelles, a scale, and a large bowl of prepared samples. After obtaining a vending license, I set up my displays and sold out in two hours. The mountain of gold turned into a mountain of green.

Picking mushrooms in America, at least in the Northeast, there is little competition. I rarely encounter another human being on my numerous summer and fall outings. One of my favorite hunting companions

*The author with her terrier Piglet, a frequent 'shrooming companion,
and freshly gathered hen of the woods*

*Halloween at Trattoria Tre Stelle. The author is at center,
dressed as a poisonous* Amanita muscaria.

was Piglet, my terrier of dubious lineage. She had overly long, thin legs, a
white, short-haired body, and a coquettish black patch over her left eye.
One ear was solid black, the other sprinkled with a poppy-seed pattern.
At the end of her back she had a round spanking spot, and under it pro-
truded an ever-active tail. A reach for the basket atop the refrigerator and
she would start howling and prancing. She even yawned from nervous-
ness lest she be left behind, which never happened! In the truck, flying
past farm fields, she would start singing and whimpering something
like "Vienna Woods," throwing her head back for optimum range. Upon
entering the woods, she would stand upright, paws on dashboard, ready
to growl at any hapless beast daring to cross the road ahead of us. Once the
door was open, Piglet would leap out of the vehicle and chase creatures
large and small. We would part company immediately; the carnivore had

no tolerance for those tedious stem-bound things I was gathering. Out of politeness we would occasionally make quick eye contact, and again she would be off chasing squirrels, chipmunks, perhaps woodchucks, or cavorting in their droppings. Hours later we would emerge, I with baskets full of multicolored mushrooms and Piglet coated in a variety of manures, both of us exhausted and utterly content. Driving home, she rode in back of the truck, reeking and pointing her nose straight into the wind.

Piglet was sixteen years old when my partner, Sarah Adams, and I opened our restaurant called Trattoria Tre Stelle. The dog and I had only one summer of 'shrooming left together.

Our restaurant specialized in wild mushroom dishes. I formalized some of my recipes, to be able to repeat them. I cooked wild mushroom pizzas from our wood-fired oven and also procured ragouts, pâtés, soups, stuffed and broiled caps, grilled buttons, batter-dipped stems. I served them with or without meat, under and over vegetables, and occasionally in omelets or crepes.

My most popular mushroom dish was also the simplest: some mixed sautéed mushrooms in olive oil and garlic, with a slice of our home-baked Tuscan bread.

Learning how to pick good edible mushrooms can be a challenge for a novice hunter. It's best to be escorted by a knowledgeable gatherer or bring your samples to someone you trust. The price might be having to share your stash, but that is a reasonable fee to pay for a correct identification.

Rain brings out mushrooms; it usually takes them three to four days to develop. They are rooted from a mycelium tentacle that runs in very long veins, deep under the soil. Mushrooms are the fruiting bodies of these veins: well over two thousand different fungi sprout forth from these gray, raggedy roots in all shapes, colors, and sizes. (A mycelium in Oregon is believed to be the largest organism on this planet.) When the conditions are favorable, a mycelium's mushrooms will pop up and thrive, but they will decline to do so in areas too cold, hot, or dry.

The volumes of printed material about mushrooms are staggering: books on the healing properties in 'shrooms, on their beneficial mineral content, on their bizarre beauty, on their culinary uniqueness. Historians have written of how the Roman emperors succumbed to their enticing aroma and flavor—and Claudius to their toxins, possibly. Many articles describe the symbiotic relationship between trees and mushrooms— for example, the beech tree and the chanterelle, the oak and the black trumpet, the apple tree and the morel—and just as one begins to subscribe to this useful information, one will find mushrooms where they ought not be. The two largest and most beautiful morels I have ever found poked through some broken macadam in the parking lot to the rear of my restaurant. I had to walk sideways to obscure their presence to two French patrons who were leaving my restaurant and had listened to my diatribe about location, location, location! So, take the mushroom-tree relationship seriously, initially, and then be more adventuresome. 'Shrooms don't always know where they belong.

The author with a platter of black trumpets

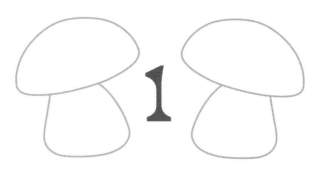

King Bolete

Boletus edulis

JUNE TO NOVEMBER

This royal species is beloved and consumed in colossal quantities in Italy as *porcino*, in France as *cep*, in Germany as *Steinpilz*, and in England as the penny bun. In European children's books, one often finds illustrations of luxuriously mossy forest floors sprouting boletes and *Amanita muscaria* (fly agarics). My memories of mushroom hunting in Germany were filled with images of dragons, Siegfried and his cronies, lakes of molten wax, small houses balanced on chicken feet, giants with twenty-foot-long beards, persuasively animated fish that talk back, abducted princesses tied to heaven-bound cliffs, and dwarves both mean and benevolent. With this many things to worry about, it was astounding I could concentrate on mushrooms at all. German woods were immaculate: there was little underbrush, all the dry lower branches were picked for kindling, and damaged trees were re-

A king bolete in nature

Freshly picked boletes

moved by foresters. In these rich, shady forests, berries and brambles had little opportunity to develop, but the handsome bolete thrived in this setting, usually under conifers or chestnuts. Their meaty stems prospered in soft spongy mosses, covered with pine-needle blankets. Pale brown baby caps would often hide a perfect tall specimen buried underneath.

In Italy they can be bought in epicurean alimentary shops, salted, dried, pickled, pureed, whole, creamed, spiced with herbs, or submerged in bottles of wines and oils. They are also available dried in large or small transparent bags, although some merchants cut up very wormy stems and hope that no one notices. In the fall, restaurants in Tuscany display signs in their windows announcing that the porcino as well as the *tartufo* (truffle) are in residence! Hot steaming tagliatelle with a generous sauce of fresh porcini can produce deep emotion. A slow-simmered soup with veal stock, wine cream, and thin-sliced boletes, such as was served in America's renowned wild mushroom restaurant, Joe's of Reading,

Boletes at an Italian market

Pennsylvania, would evoke similar euphoria. Alas, this Polish family-run enterprise closed its doors in 1997. In Russia the celebrated *borovik* is the autumnal staple of many a table. In his memoir *Speak, Memory*, Vladimir Nabokov provides us with the typical Slavic recipe, which calls for mounds of sour cream and fresh dill.

I vividly recall my best bolete hunt. A few weeks prior to opening our restaurant in 1994, Sarah and I stayed in a tiny rented cottage in the Adirondacks, near Moose Lake. One morning early we rented a canoe and began paddling around a large pond, close to shore. A few minutes later I succumbed to hysterics. On the left side the whole long shore, under a canopy of pines, had erupted with young *Boletus edulis*, a totally breathtaking sight. We paddled back to the old stone inn, barged into their kitchen, gathered up their largest pots and pans, and returned to collect the abundant offerings. The much-admired bounty was shared with all.

In the hilltop villages of the Val d'Orcia in southern Tuscany, there are excellent trattorias serving pecorino cheese, big red wines, pici pasta, truffle oil, and wild boar carpaccio, as well as, of course, porcini! The largest frying pan I have ever seen was in a small hamlet near Monte Amiata

ASSOCIAZIONE MICOLOGICA "BRESADOLA"

GRUPPO DI AREZZO
DELEGAZIONE ALTA VALTIBERINA
PIEVE SANTO STEFANO (AR)
CON IL PATROCINIO DI:

COMUNE DI PIEVE SANTO STEFANO
COMUNITÀ MONTANA VALTIBERINA TOSCANA

7ª MOSTRA MICOLOGICA

28 Settembre dalle ore 15.00 alle ore 22.00
29 Settembre dalle ore 10.00 alle ore 22.00

PIEVE SANTO STEFANO (AR)
Ex Asilo Umberto 1°

A poster for a bolete festival in Arezzo, Italy

called Vivo D'Orcia; this local shop–welded wonder, sitting on a bed of hot coals, was twenty feet in circumference and extended a twelve-foot handle. Sputtering in a generous bath of olive oil were mixed cut boletes, served with robust Tuscan bread. The circular wave of hungry enthusiasts weaving around the pan, wine in cups, felt like some mysterious ritual from an early century. When cooking, I have observed that a large quantity of a given ingredient can actually improve the flavor. What this enormous vessel delivered in aroma, flavor, and appearance was simply wonderful! This yearly event is called Sagra del Fungo (or "festival of the mushroom"), and it never occurred to me not to hasten back to it as well as the entire Val d'Orcia, which was named a UNESCO World Heritage Site in 2004.

Boletes have a unique earthy flavor, and they rarely require more than a wipedown with a damp paper towel, the lighter the better. If there is dirt at the base of the stem, this can be scraped off, preserving as much as possible.

Ristorante Tre Scalini in Rome prepares porcini grilled, brushed with olive oil, salt, and lemon. I like to grill them this way, too, and sometimes I add ripe red pearl tomatoes to the skewers for color and flavor. I set the skewers close to the hot embers of a charcoal grill and sear the mushrooms lightly on all sides. (It's best to leave the smaller buttons whole and cut the larger specimens in half lengthwise—the 'shrooms are less apt to fall off the skewer if pierced through both cap and stem.) Grilled boletes work very well on (also grilled) steak, chicken, or, if a vegetarian direction is preferred, well-seasoned pasta, potatoes, or rice.

The following recipe is a good way to enjoy boletes when the quantities often found in Italy are not available locally.

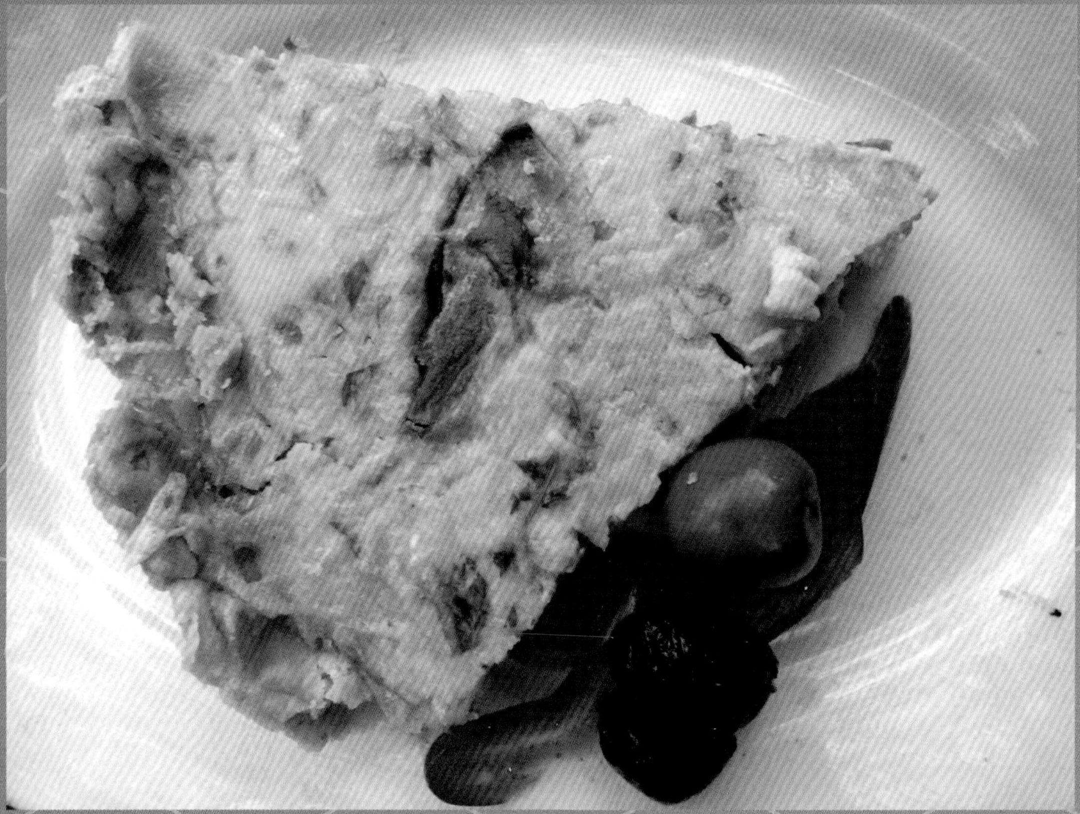

Bolete Custard Tart

Serves 4 to 6

- Pâte brisée (flaky pastry) dough for 10½-inch tart pan, refrigerated
- 2 or 3 medium-large *Boletus* caps and stems
- 2 teaspoons butter
- 2 teaspoons olive oil
- 2 cups milk
- 3 egg yolks
- ½ teaspoon salt
- ½ teaspoon white pepper
- ½ teaspoon grated nutmeg
- 2 tablespoons fresh parsley, finely chopped
- Garnishes such as oil-cured olives and raw pepper slices

Roll out the dough and transfer it to a 10½-inch tart pan. Line the dough with foil and beans to weigh it down and bake in a preheated 375°F oven for about 10 to 15 minutes, just enough to see the shell begin to lightly brown. Remove it from the oven to cool.

Slice the boletes into ⅛-inch thick pieces. Gently sauté in butter and olive oil until they are soft, approximately 5 to 7 minutes.

For the filling, combine the milk, egg yolks, salt, pepper, nutmeg, and parsley. Add the cooked mushrooms and pour the filling into the cooled pastry shell.

Bake in a preheated 375°F oven for approximately 20 minutes. The filling should be firm and showing a light golden color.

2

Chanterelle

Cantharellus cibarius (Europe) & closely related American species

LATE JUNE TO SEPTEMBER

Look for them, sometimes as early as the end of June, under beeches; in mixed woods around clay deposits; near culverts, bridges, and stream banks. They are a cheerful, socially inclined species. Spot one, and you will usually find dozens. Their size ranges from small buttons to large tea saucers. The shape tends to become fluted, with casual gills descending down the slender and tapered stem. Their color varies from pale yellow to a robust orange (free-range chicken) egg yolk. Cut in half, the flesh exposed is ivory. One of the strongest clues to their identification is their faint smell of saddle soap—some 'shroomers describe it as apricot, which sounds more alluring. Often chanterelles will erupt in long veins, so prolific you could fill a basket in minutes. They are perhaps the best beginner's mushroom, easy to identify, plentiful, and absolutely delicious! One year, when they ar-

Chanterelles from the author's first picking in July 2021

A trio of chanterelles in nature

rived really early, I inspected all my reliable spots, and saw babies everywhere. Committing infanticide was not the right thing to do (although the buttons are wonderful and crunchy pickled in a fresh herb marinade). When I returned after the Fourth of July, they had progressed to the most complimentary proportions, three- to five-inch caps with long and elegant gams.

Having already written about my most lucrative chanterelle hunt in the introduction, I would just like to add that of all the edible mushrooms I have bagged (except for the *Grifola frondosa*, a.k.a. hen of the woods), it's the chanterelle I continue to find year after year in the same locations, in huge quantities.

A dry season though, for any species, is utterly disappointing. Summers like that make me morose, as I ponder over what to do with myself... take up knitting, aimlessly canoe around Cayuga Lake, or watch reruns of *Foyle's War*? None of these activities can match a long and lucrative mushroom hunt!

Sectioned chanterelles

The only time I got "wounded" in the woods was when I attempted to coax baby chanterelles out of their leafy beds, to produce the stem as well as the cap with my index finger. Inadvertently, I poked my finger into the parlor of a brown widow spider. In a grumpy mood, as usual, the widow bit me in my fingertip. I assumed it was a bee sting, but two days later the finger turned blackish blue and swelled up to twice its size. Luckily my doctor was well informed about the potency of this arachnid and put me on antibiotics in the nick of time. A short time later, I was 'shrooming again.

Saveur magazine published two of my chanterelle recipes in their July/August 1999 issue, to accompany an article by Eric Goodman about foraging in the Finger Lakes. One of them was for the following soup, which I still love to make.

Chanterelle Soup

Serves 4 to 6

- 3 tablespoons extra virgin olive oil
- 8 ounces (4 cups) of fresh chanterelles, trimmed and sliced thinly
- ½ red onion, diced small
- 2 or 3 cloves of garlic, minced
- ½ cup Finger Lakes chardonnay
- 5 cups chicken stock
- 1 cup packed, coarsely chopped dandelion greens or escarole
- Touch of fresh oregano
- 1 teaspoon white wine vinegar
- Salt and freshly ground black pepper
- Green onions (wild if possible), minced
- Freshly grated Parmigiano Reggiano cheese

In a 4- or 5-quart heavy enameled pot, cook the olive oil over moderate heat. Sweat the chanterelles and red onion in the oil until the mushrooms begin to give up their juices and brown a bit.

Add minced garlic and sauté for 2 minutes, and then add the chardonnay and give it a few minutes more to cook off the alcohol.

Add the chicken stock and bring to a simmer. (Other stocks also work well, such as mushroom stock or a homemade vegetable stock of dandelion greens and oregano.)

Add vinegar, salt, and pepper to taste; sprinkle with green onions; and serve hot, passing Parmigiano Reggiano at the table.

3

Caesar's Mushroom

Amanita caesarea (Europe) & *Amanita jacksonii* (North America)

JULY TO OCTOBER

Amycologist's dream come true! The Caesar is a magnificent-looking fungus and tastes as good as it looks. The Roman emperors, whom it was named after, supposedly cherished it. It maintains its regal appellation throughout Europe: *impériale* in French, *cesarski* in Polish, and *Kaiserling* in German.

My heart always skips a beat when I come upon a stand of stately Caesars. They grow under mixed trees in acid ground and can maintain a tall (six to eight inch) stature, but are even better when captured in infancy, as *ovolini* (little eggs), as the Italians call them. When tiny, they are tightly draped in a pure white skin, and as they grow, the bright red oval cap breaks through the epidermis. Once standing, the cap sheds its protective enclosure to reveal bright yellow gills, a yellow stem and ring, and a bulbous base retaining some of the white veil. At first the cap

Sliced Caesars—a mixture of young ovolini and mature specimens—on a bed of greens

A sectioned ovolino, or immature Caesar

Caesar ovolini in nature. The red caps have begun to burst through the white skin.

remains hemispherical and then upon maturing flattens out. In damp weather, the cap feels a little gelatinous. When cap and stem are cut open, the interior reveals a creamy white color, and in an older specimen the stem can become tubular.

I must admit that the first time I tasted a tiny morsel of the *Amanita caesarea* I was highly apprehensive, never having encountered one in the post–World War II years in Germany and Switzerland. All my 'shroom books years later highly recommended it, though, as long as you don't mix in its cousin *Amanita phalloides* (the death cap), as Agrippina supposedly did to finish off her husband, Claudius. (Being the incestuous sister of Caligula and mother of the ungifted Nero perhaps gives one some license to kill, however.) That first nibble was very fine, and I have been enjoying this mushroom ever since.

Amateur 'shroomers should be careful with this mushroom because it is one of the few edible ones in the most evil of genera, the *Amanita*, but if, for example, you lay the poisonous *Amanita muscaria* (fly agaric) next to a Caesar all resemblance ceases. The fly agaric has a bright red cap with small, snowflake-like warts, a long white stem, and white cuticles expanding into a bulb at the base. For centuries peasants in Russia (prior to flypaper) cut the fly agaric into small pieces and set them out with some water in saucers on windowsills. Flies drank the water with the desired results. As I write in the introduction, know your poisonous mushrooms first, and then little by little drift toward the edible ones—it's well worth it.

My largest summoning of Caesars happened at La Foce, the estate of the writer Iris Origo (1902–1988) in the Val d'Orcia. Sarah and I had been invited to stay in one of the fine smaller houses (a *casa colonica*, or farmhouse) now owned by the author's daughters. Ms. Origo's gardens, including the cypress-edged serpentine road ascending in front of her estate, are among the most photographed views in Tuscany. With the help of architect and landscape designer Cecil Pinsent, Origo also collaborated on many other projects, including the restoration of the estate's main villa (a former fifteenth-century inn), a school and hospital for the local *contadini*, a chapel, and a cemetery, as well as fountains, pergolas, and grand staircases topped with urns. Much of this was built and carved in local travertine, a type of limestone. This part of Tuscany has peculiar soil, a dusty white, powdery *creta*, or clay. Antonio Origo struggled for years to make his over 3,000 acres of farm fields fertile and obedient—it took a long time.

During World War II, the Nazis occupied La Foce and imprisoned

The twelve ages of Caesar

English soldiers there. The Origos themselves saved many local and refugee children by marching them way up the hill to Montalcino, safer territory, away from Allied bombings. Much of the estate had to be rebuilt or repaired after the war.

One morning early at La Foce, hand-woven willow basket in hand, I entered the oak forest behind our rented farmhouse. The ground under the oak trees was thick with saplings, bushes, and tall, prickly weeds, but I emerged a short hour later, leaves in hair, scratches on hands and fingers, and basket lined in neat rows of orange glory. Our local cleaning lady was

A mature Caesar in nature

just finishing a few chores when I came barging in, disheveled but beaming. She stared into the basket. I could see she was quite impressed. She proclaimed the mushrooms to be *molto buoni* and also added that she was surprised that an American would know about these Caesars!

Raw Caesar Platter

Serves 4 to 6

- 6 to 8 ounces arugula
- 6 to 8 Caesar's mushrooms
- Salt and pepper
- 1 large clove of garlic, minced
- Parmesan cheese, shaved
- Olive oil
- 1 to 2 teaspoons lemon juice
- Fresh Italian parsley, minced

The best way to cook this mushroom is . . . not to. It's absolutely delicious raw! When I am blessed with a good gathering of Caesars, I edit out the older ones and the tougher stems for soup, pâté, or sauces, but the remaining darlings are destined for this Caesar platter. The platter should be outrageously large and the dinner company very special.

Arrange a layer of young arugula on a platter. You will have something to show off here! After the Caesars have had their wipedown, cut them in thin slices from top to bottom. Assemble a layer of the thin slices atop the greens. Salt and pepper them lightly and add minced garlic. Shave parmesan and a sprinkle of olive oil and lemon juice. Build up layer after layer, six to eight in all, and let the assemblage rest at least 3 to 4 hours before serving as an appetizer. Garnish with parsley.

This is a handsomely colorful dish and usually receives *oohs* and *aahs* from dinner guests, followed by *mmms* and *yums*.

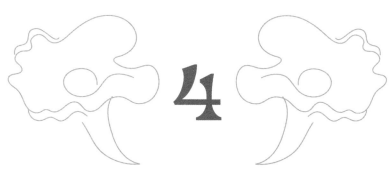

4

Black Trumpet or Horn of Plenty

Craterellus cornucopioides (Europe) & Craterellus fallax (North America)

JULY TO OCTOBER

This is my favorite mushroom in America. In Italy it is called the "poor man's truffle," and in France it is known as the "black trumpet of death." Clever verbiage used by those cunning French who want the horn of plenty all to themselves. This is a blackish gray mushroom that thrives under oak trees and stumps and appears just a week or two after its golden cousin the chanterelle thins out. When provided with a rich, acidic soil and generous moisture, it will appear in colossal families. The aroma of the horn does evoke the deep, complex scent of the overpriced but not overrated black truffle. Its flavor is hard to describe, because it is truly unique. When I made horn of plenty

The author with a platter of black trumpets

Black trumpets in nature

Three black trumpets at various stages of growth

and arugula pizzas in my wood-fired oven, the customer line would start winding around the restaurant in prolific circles.

The only problem with this mushroom is finding it. It is uniquely skilled at "hide-and-seek." When it first emerges, it looks exactly as described: like a small, perfectly shaped black trumpet. But as it matures, it takes on a more irregular and wrinkled appearance, with grayish tones, allowing it to blend in very successfully with curled-up dead oak leaves. On many occasions I have stood up to my ankles in a family of trumpets, unaware of their immediate presence.

Almost always they appear in large numbers, and as a rule, if you find a few, they are there. Be patient, walk slowly between the oak stumps and trees, and really focus on the fallen leaves. Don't let them fool you!

Once you find them, and see how and where they grow in relation to oak trees, filling a basket should take no time at all. Cleaning and preparation is easy as well. Snip the bottom of the slender stem with scissors, which will remove any attached dirt, and take a quick glance at the trumpet tube for any uninvited occupants. Mostly they are quite unobstructed by insects or soil. Once lightly rinsed, they reveal their beautiful shapes... glossy black musical instruments, small and large.

Like so much former European peasant fare, the horn of plenty today is served in three-star restaurants as a highly desirable epicurean triumph. The gentlest simmering in butter or olive oil releases heavenly aromas from black trumpets. Their flavor is voluptuous and complex. The serving spoons should not be too generous. This mushroom is good also for freezing, drying, or pulverizing.

I like to prepare black trumpets fresh and serve them over polenta, as in the following recipe. The mound of polenta, being a fine gold color, looks most handsome with the glistening black trumpets at its center.

Black Trumpets with Polenta

Serves 4 to 6

- 2 cups cooked firm polenta
- 8 ounces black trumpets
- 2 tablespoons butter
- 1 teaspoon salt
- ½ cup heavy cream
- Fresh parsley or cilantro, chopped
- Grated Parmesan, if desired

While the polenta is cooking, trim the tip of the trumpets' stems and cut them in half. Sauté them with butter and salt on a low flame for approximately 15 minutes or until they are soft but still hold their shape.

Slowly add cream to the mushrooms and stir.

Ladle the polenta onto a prewarmed serving platter. Create a small "bowl" in the center of the polenta to hold the mushroom sauce for serving.

Add the fresh herbs and cheese.

OUTINGS

❈

Saturday, June 8

Rain, light thunder, more rain. All radio stations, especially the religious ones, predict more of the same for days to come. What to do? I have to be in the woods to greet the early chanterelles that I left behind a few days ago. Can't drive the "Carlotta" (2004 VW Passat) again; she has barely three inches of snout clearance under her front bumper, so she'll get stuck in the first puddle. I look at Hank Jr., my 1992 Ford Ranger, a faithful, dependable vehicle, but unfortunately not a four-wheel-drive model. Ballast is what is needed; surely with extra weight we will get in and out of the forest okay. I look around the Trumansburg estate, evaluating potential weights.... Aha, there they are, two cast-iron Kohler sinks, in matching avocado green porcelain and very heavy indeed! With some panting and puffing, I load the sinks near the tailgate of the truck and add a sledgehammer along with three flower pots, still full of last year's potting soil.... We have weight! (The sinks have recently been evicted from our remodeled bathroom, which had to be relieved of its banal 1970s decor.) It is early in the morning, I've had coffee, Hank has gas, and my usual hunting gear is on the passenger seat.

The landscape has changed dramatically from my previous outings. This month the weeds are aspiring to be bushes, all roadside ditches are filled with brownish water, and the pockmarked macadam shows cracks and holes filled with murky liquid.

Everyone is sleeping late this morning. The field grazers are still resting, cars are parked in garages and on driveways, and the forever-busy rodents have not begun crossing the highway at inopportune times. I plot my route prior to entering the drenched woods: the concept is to enter higher and then descend toward the lower paths, so Hank Jr. will not have to attempt to ascend a rutty, muddy hill. Also, on a somewhat higher plateau is where I left the baby chanterelles. The truck struggles as soon as we leave asphalt, and in low gear, I slide very slowly and stop in some soft mud. Today is a day for tedious slogging on foot. The quantity of gold buttons in the soft, mossy ground is staggering, and they have grown very nicely in four days. Now they have reached the diameter of a dollar coin. All the lively mushroom families, however, are inundated with long beige slugs. Chanterelles seldom host slugs, so what is going on? Of course, it's self-explanatory—the incontinent rain has turned the forest floor into one big sliding rink, and the usually cumbersome slug can move hither and yonder with the greatest of ease. And does. The gathering takes a little more time this morning, for the gastropod mollusks have to be picked off the mushroom caps and stems. After an hour of intense gathering and picking, my handmade Italian basket (sold at farmers' markets in the Chianti region) is full of firm and aromatic chanterelles. Most mushroom gatherers claim this species releases a pleasant aroma of apricots, but I also detect a faint waft of saddle soap.

Saturday, June 15

A glorious spring morning. I'm up at five as usual, brewing coffee and heating milk. Our "closet queen" Scooch is released from his voluntary night quarters, namely Sarah's long and deep closet. The terrier-cum-schnauzer (a successful mix) prefers the space to his padded crate. How I wish we could go mushroom hunting together, but he still yearns to be in Ohio and I can't trust him. Basket, knife, Vicks VapoRub, extra shirt . . . all is in Carlotta the Passat, ready to go. I named her Carlotta because she's "alotta" car—this supremely engineered vehicle indulges in endless bells and whistles. She moans and groans about trivia: an open trunk, an unfastened seatbelt (imagine in the forest), an ebbing supply of gas, or a passenger exiting while she is still creeping ahead!

I'm on the road at last, fortified by two coffees and a brisk shower. After ten days of rain and leaden sky, the sun has finally emerged. The narrow two-lane road is glowing with light and cheerfulness. Even the long yellow passing stripes are dancing on the undulating surface of the asphaltic gray. I am tempted to pass, but there is no one in front of me. All the trees, bushes, and fields are gratefully green, replenished by the steady falling water. The passing wheat fields are standing a proud two foot high, and there are still clusters of white daisies left, and patches of gold butter-flies as well as an occasional brilliant orange poppy. Carlotta enters the woods, I disentangle myself from the seatbelt by sitting on it, the radio is turned off, and all windows are rolled open. One doesn't just see mush-rooms, one also smells them, along with many other delightful woodsy fragrances.

I park near one of my most lucrative chanterelle spots, and then pro-ceed to advance, under some very low-growing branches, into the forest, which is a dense stand of poplars and birches, as well as an occasional large oak.

Nothing has emerged from the mycological world except for a few poi-sonous *Amanita citrina*, pretty enough, but definitely not for the table. Usually, a week prior to a general arrival, this location will preview the hunts to come. Minute, adorable chanterelles nest here ahead of any other spot, but not today. Well, the nights have been too cool. After this disappointment, I stroll around a nearby grove of poplars, where oyster mushrooms tend to congregate, even in the spring. But all I see are a few tired clusters, hanging dejectedly. A slow cruise back home past yards and fields also reveals nothing of interest.

The author cleaning chanterelles

5
Slippery Jack
& Tamarack Jack

Suillus luteus &
Suillus grevillei

AUGUST TO OCTOBER

These two plentiful and underrated mushrooms make their debut late in summer, typically at the end of August, and, the weather cooperating, fruit consistently well into October. After a thorough rainfall, they will emerge in hordes. Of all the mushrooms I have gathered, none are more symbiotically related to trees than the jacks. *Suillus grevillei* flourishes under tamaracks, which have a wide growth range among American conifers. The *luteus* prefers Scotch pines, but will also pop up on banks and along edges of footpaths (as long as pines are nearby). The jacks have innumerable first cousins, and equally many tedious names to describe them: chicken fat mushroom, hollow bolete, variegated bolete, granulated bolete, sticky bolete... enough already! I have not ever come across a suspicious *Suillus* in my considerable collection of guidebooks or in person.

*Freshly picked
slippery jacks*

A slippery jack in nature

Mother Nature provides an interesting disguise to *Suillus grevillei*. When this mushroom arrives, the needles of the tamarack tree turn a pale yellow for the winter months. Descending pine needles, yellow, settle on the sticky yellow caps of the desired crop. It is not unlike looking for black trumpets amid curled-up oak leaves of remarkably similar color. But where would be the adventure of picking mushrooms if not for these challenges?

The outer skin on the caps of *Suillus* tends to be very gelatinous and sticky, which can translate into a slimy mass when cooked. But when I add these 'shrooms to a pâté, I leave the skin on. It helps congeal the pâté, and an hour in a hot oven dries out the sticky surface. In general, *Suillus* do not have a deep or distinctive flavor, but they are very social and like to be part of many dishes: pasta sauces, omelets, soups, etc. They relate very well to pork products … especially crisp fried bacon. Infant jacks are delicious fried whole—no need to trim off the excess spongy material from the bottom of the caps … or worry about the top.

One morning at sunup in the pretty hilltop village of Pienza in the Val d'Orcia in southern Tuscany, I saw women lifting wooden buckets loaded with slippery jacks onto open trucks. They were headed to a nearby farmer's market. The caps of the freshly picked jacks were peeled clean. The women explained that they could not place the mushrooms into containers unpeeled because they would stick together, impossible to separate or set into scales for the desired amounts. They had accomplished all this picking and cleaning in just two hours, rising at 4 a.m. to be ready to load the trucks by 6, and an hour or so after that, they saw their golden ware beautifully laid out and sorted by size under umbrellas or in tents. By noontime their treasure had been hoarded off into various Tuscan kitchens, pantries, and trattorias.

The gifted Bohemian physician and mycologist Julius Vincenz von Krombholz, born in 1782 and educated in Prague, wrote a book entitled *Illustrations and Descriptions from Nature about Mushrooms Which Are Edible, Poisonous, and Suspect*, featuring truly marvelous hand-colored engravings. To the members of the genus *Suillus*, which he calls "boletes," Krombholz gives names like "yellow buttercup"—so far, so good—but then he goes on to label them "swine mushrooms." (An appellation that has stuck: *Suillus* means "of swine.") And it gets worse: he dubs the slippery jack *Ziengenlippen* … "goat lips"! Do sit down for a bowl of sautéed goat lips and see how many dinner guests will be returning.

I had an unexpected and quite rewarding mushroom episode in the city of Rovinj, Croatia. Formerly named Rovigno, and then a part of Italy, this dreamy small city sits right on the still-pristine Istrian coast of the Adriatic Sea. We had rented a small apartment in the lower, oldest part of the city. We walked under a fourteenth-century stone arch to enter this ancient district. There was no view onto the sea, and the windows were, as typical, very small, but they did reveal an inner courtyard, crisscrossed with laundry lines, and on our windowsills rotund pigeons and more slender doves demanding handouts. Everything felt and looked Italian, but everyone was Slavic. … I have never felt more at home in any country. This was our second trip to Croatia. We had already marveled at the built glories of Dubrovnik and Split as well as the natural beauty of islands Korčula, Hvar, and Brač. Our intention was to spend a few days in Rovinj. We ended up staying three weeks. Here was one reason why.

A basket of slippery jacks. Note grass adhering.

One morning we walked to the north of the lower city and came upon a small seaquarium cum bookstore and museum. I noticed a steep hill and tall pines rising in back of this building. After we had observed local as well as exotic sea creatures cavorting in clean tanks, browsed through picture books, and purchased a map or two, we were ready to head back to old town.

But the hill could not be left pining. A scramble up the steep grade brought us to a mini-park with two paths crossing, surrounded by very tall, long-needled pines. The needles had formed a thick mat, and poking up through the debris . . . a sizable and handsome family of *Suillus grevillei*! Maps were folded and buried in pockets, providing us with two strong bags for our gathering. With the help of Sarah (long resigned to my uncontrollable eccentricities), I gathered the crop quickly. As we were unlocking our tiny medieval kitchen, our landlady, who lived directly across from us, came out with her pointy-snouted dog, Joska, and smiled at what was protruding at the top of our bags.

Inspired by the simple but extremely tasty local concoction of greens and potatoes called *mangold* (probably an Austrian dish), I mixed the butter-browned jacks with sliced boiled potatoes and fresh spinach. Then, I added more olive oil as well as a shot of *slivovice* (plum brandy). These goings-on brought out our diminutive but lively landlady again, still with Joska, and they were both very happy to have a generous sampling of the "new improved" *mangold*. She returned a short hour later with a platter of homemade sweet biscuits filled with dried fruits, berries, and a shot of *slivovice* binding it all.

Slippery Jack Skewers

Serves 4 to 6

- 1 pound slippery jacks and/or tamarack jacks
- Vegetables suitable for grilling, such as tomatoes, zucchini, and peppers
- Olive oil
- Salt and pepper

After collecting a generous amount of these mushrooms, which tend to grow in large groupings, select a pound or so of the younger ones that have firmer caps and sponges. Wipe the stems and caps clean with a damp cloth to remove leaves, grass, and soil. Trim the lower part of the stem.

Carefully spear the mushrooms on presoaked wooden skewers. They interlock very well with small tomatoes, zucchini wedges, and gold peppers. When putting the mushrooms onto the skewers, insert them thoroughly to the outer rim of the cap. This will help in keeping all of the participants compacted together through the grilling process.

Brush the skewered jacks with olive oil, sprinkle liberally with salt and pepper, and place on a hot charcoal grill. Lightly cook the mushrooms on all sides to a crisp, light brown color.

Serve on Italian bread or rice.

6

Morel

Morchella esculenta and related species

MAY

I f the *Boletus edulis* is the king of mushrooms, then the *Morchella esculenta* should be coroneted as the queen or perhaps, given its wrinkled, elderly visage, the queen mother. No two mushrooms could be more different in appearance. The rotundly robust bolete, not unlike King Henry the Eighth, and the scrawny, wrinkled morel . . . perhaps Queen Victoria in her black shrouds and laces of "forever mourning." The morel is an early riser, arriving in May; the bolete takes its time and gets up later in the summer. Both are celebrated around the world for their culinary rewards. Both are also excellent for drying: they reconstitute extremely well in warm water or broth.

The *esculenta* can have a round or elongated head. The light brown, hole-riddled head or cap fuses with the pale cream, stringy stem, bonding into an integral whole. The mushroom is completely hollow from cap

Freshly picked morels

Halved morels showing their hollow interiors

through stem, and often it will house lodgers—insects, slugs, etc. Related types of morel, the "black," the "thick-footed," and the *conica*, are also highly comestible. Most cookbooks recommend blanching them prior to eating. I have never followed that advice, and see no particular need to, but I do simmer them for eight to ten minutes.

Some domestically grown morels are available, but they don't have the same depth of flavor as the wild ones—so get out there and hunt! The morel's distinctive hole-riddled appearance makes the search easier. Find one or two and have the patience to look further. They tend to congregate, particularly around apple trees and orchards.

One spring in the early 1980s, Sarah and I were staying in northern Italy when an invitation arrived from Annecy, the "Venice of France." A staff member of Tufts University's study abroad program invited us for a short sojourn in this small city at the very edge of beautiful Lake Annecy in southeast France. Having just been to the Italian Venice, we felt another version of that visual mirage would be most delightful. Tufts had the good sense to quarter its school in an ancient nunnery, and yes, there was an old apple orchard in back of the structure. After an extensive exploration of the delights of the region of Annecy, edged by the Rhône and the Alps, we then turned our attention to the city's built environment: the early arched stone bridges, twelfth-century castles, inner waterways, and winding, narrow pedestrian walkways. I read that evening in one of our English guidebooks that this location had an 89 percent humidity rating. The day before, we had watched teenage daredevils in airborne contraptions skydive from a steep cliff high above Lake Annecy. Now I was contemplating a more earthbound adventure.

In the moist morning, still foggy, I drifted into the old orchard. A few young apple trees had been planted, but mostly the trunks were cracked and gray with their broken crowns trying to reroot themselves. I had brought neither knife nor basket but did have a spring jacket on. Being a

A quartet of morels in nature

The author with two large morels

newcomer here, I followed sound advice. Walk to the end of the orchard along one edge with eyes seriously focused on the ground, turn around, move over three to four feet, and repeat. The orchard laid out a deep carpet of decayed apples, cores, leaves, and branches. When I completed my disciplined exercise, I had gently cradled in my jacket almost a dozen *Morchella esculenta*!

Kitchen, gas stove, cast iron pan, butter, a wooden spoon followed in quick order. The cleaned and quartered morels slid from cutting board into pan. A few slugs had been evicted (although the French would probably not have objected to their presence, in butter no less). The aromatic and delicate concoction in the pan was placed on thin-sliced crunchy baguette and topped with fleur de sel and dried thyme. We opened a bottle of champagne even though it was only ten in the morning.

I have to admit, though, that the morel has eluded me more often than not. I do not recall hauling large amounts out of the woods or from the fields. Occasionally I have had success, a dozen or so, here or there, mostly when least expected. It was most annoying to read about the Frenchmen who boarded a plane to the U.S. in May 1981, one year after Mount St. Helens spewed ashes over half of Washington State. The Gallic opportunists gathered hundreds of pounds of morels that had sprung up from the mineral-rich ash. They must have bought dehydrators for their motel rooms to have gotten such bounty back to their own country. (Perhaps they bribed the customs inspectors?)

When Sarah and I decided to downsize our lifestyle, we looked for a new home in the nearby village of Trumansburg, New York. For me the real estate deal was done when I walked around the large pond and yard, and under a slick cottonwood tree found a single very tall and elegant morel!

Morels in Cream Sauce over Pasta

Serves 4

- 1 small white onion, thinly sliced
- 3 to 4 tablespoons unsalted butter
- 1 teaspoon salt
- 12 morels, quartered and rinsed
- 2 tablespoons dry white wine
- 1 cup heavy cream
- ¾ pound Italian pasta, preferably a wide noodle like tagliatelle
- ¼ teaspoon white pepper
- ¼ cup of fresh Italian parsley, minced
- Finely grated Parmesan cheese, if desired

Thinly slice the onion and sauté with salt and 1 to 2 tablespoons of butter. Set aside.

Delicately simmer the cleaned morels in 1 to 2 tablespoons of butter, and add wine. Once the mushrooms are softened, in approximately 5 minutes, add the onions and cream. Cook on low flame for 8 to 10 minutes or until the ingredients are assimilated.

Pour the sauce over ¾ pound of Italian pasta, such as pappardelle, cooked al dente. Add white pepper and minced parsley, and serve on warmed plates. Finely grated Parmesan cheese can be added if desired.

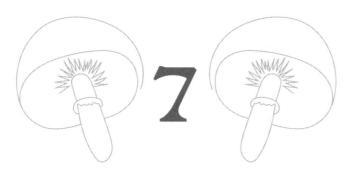

7

Meadow Mushroom

Agaricus campestris

SEPTEMBER TO NOVEMBER

Nineteen sixty-two was a good year. The College of Art and Architecture at Cornell University decided to take me in with a full scholarship, including room and board. When I arrived in early September, though, I was informed that the first check would not be available until the end of the month. My modest one-room apartment with kitchen privileges, far below Cayuga's waters, on Seneca Street, was a long way from campus, but my daily walk to school took me through a historic cemetery green with vegetation and white with the caps and buttons of meadow mushrooms.

Once again, the fungus to the rescue! I conned my German landlady into a small loan, and after procuring a loaf of rye bread as well as a pound of butter, I made myself a large panful of fried *Agaricus*. That's how the next three weeks went, rye bread with mushrooms on top, or rye bread

Freshly picked meadow mushrooms

Meadow mushrooms in nature

with mushrooms on the side, and the grand finale, mushrooms in bread-crumbs, fried in butter. My spirits were sinking as I sat on a bench in front of Franklin Hall on campus contemplating my predictable dinner.

Just then an outgoing and approachable professor of art walked by and asked what I thought about Cornell. Professor H. Peter Kahn had a pronounced German accent and mine was Baltic-Russian, and we recognized the emigrant in each other immediately. This led to the usual where, when, and how. Professor Kahn had emigrated to America in the nick of time, before the Nazis locked the gates. His father's tenure as conductor of the Stuttgart Symphony Orchestra was over, but he quickly resumed his musical career in the United States by conducting the music for the Ballet Russe di Monte Carlo and got to travel extensively. Peter Kahn enlisted in the U.S. Army as a private and was later promoted to sergeant.

At the Nuremberg Trials, Peter served as translator, being proficient in both German and English. On a lighter note, though, the professor recalled decorating General Patton's personal jeep. Among Peter's many talents was also very fine calligraphy, and the immodest general insisted that his military status be clearly signaled by his name and his four stars lettered in gold leaf on both doors of the vehicle.

Since Professor Kahn and I also shared the city of Hamburg as our former base, there was a lot more to chat about. After some lively discussions, including architecture, bridges, Chancellor Bismarck, painting, favorite museums, and German cuisine, we also discovered that we were fellow mycologists. I explained to Peter how monotonous my diet had been. That did it! I was immediately invited to dinner at his house, and he even made me a hand-drawn map to a village called Dryden. A few hours later, I roared off toward Dryden on my 250cc BMW. The pre-helmet days of New York State added to my feeling of euphoria. Half an hour later the motorcycle and I found ourselves just outside the village and in front of a large, well-proportioned farmhouse filled with Kahns, nine to be exact.

Professor Peter and his wife Ruthie (already a renowned author of children's books such as *My Father's Dragon*) had procured seven daughters. The table was set, Herr Professor was fussing in the kitchen, and I met the family, which took a little time. When Peter reemerged from the kitchen with a pile of bread and an even more considerable pile of fried *Agaricus campestris*, I began to succumb to major gravity. How could this be happening—what mortal sin had I committed?

Waftings from the stove confirmed, though, that this would be just the appetizer, and the highly esteemed Kahn rump roast stew would follow quickly. The well-spiced, slow-simmered concoction, filled with healing vegetables and red wine, was generously ladled over little potatoes. This most satisfying nourishment restored my faith in humanity as well as responding to chance meetings. The entire Kahn clan and I bonded for life, and ate mushrooms together many more times.

The meadow mushroom, first cultivated in caves in France by the "Sun King" Louis XIV, is the true ancestor of our store-bought white buttons as well as the larger portobello. It is a gilled mushroom with a white cap, skirt, and stem. On a young specimen the gills are pink to light brown, and as the 'shroom gets older the gills evolve into a deeper rich brown. Since the destroying angel (*Amanita bisporigera*) resembles the meadow mushroom, and also dresses in all white, do not pick white-gilled specimens—they could be poisonous! Also, carefully examine the base of the mushroom: the evil one grows from a bulbous cup, the good one does not.

The meadow mushroom is easy to find and can be very plentiful, and its flavor surpasses that of its basket-bound, plastic-wrapped commercial offspring, nourished by bales of mulch and manure.

After my cemetery mushroom dependency was forgotten, I enjoyed the *Agaricus* again, and the Cornell campus, with its many parks and nature

A trio of meadow mushrooms at different stages of growth

walks, provided well-stocked hunting grounds. A classmate of mine served me a very tasty *Agaricus* appetizer, which I still recall: medium caps brushed with olive oil and filled with a mixture of spicy ground pork sausage, breadcrumbs, garlic, and egg, topped with grated parmesan. These dainty mounds were then broiled until crusty and bubbly on top and served with braised greens and Chianti—one hardly needed more!

In the summer, when cooking our burgers outside, I score the large mushroom caps, coat them lightly in olive oil, add salt and pepper, grill them to a rich, slightly charred color, and place them atop the burger with a slice of onion. The smaller caps love to be stuffed with a slice of pork (or chicken) sausage and then broiled in a baking oven to a light golden brown. A cube of smoked Gouda cheese also hits the mark.

The really large caps with tougher skins can serve a utilitarian purpose

The same trio, gills up

if finely chopped or thinly sliced and then added to sauces, meatloaves, soups, or stuffing.

The meadow mushroom also has the reputation of being one of the safest of all edible fungi. So, enjoying it thinly sliced raw is another option. In salads with lettuce, cucumbers, hard-boiled eggs, radishes . . . why stop now? Enjoy!

Meadow Mushrooms on Potato Pancakes

Serves 4 to 6

- 4 large Yukon gold potatoes, grated
- 2 large eggs
- 3 tablespoons breadcrumbs
- Salt and pepper
- ½ pound meadow mushrooms
- 2 tablespoons butter
- 1 tablespoon olive oil
- 2 to 3 tablespoons sour cream
- Cilantro or parsley
- 1 sliced red onion, if desired

Combine the potatoes, eggs, and breadcrumbs, with salt and pepper to taste, and panfry 4 to 6 medium-size crispy potato pancakes. (Yukon gold potatoes offer the best flavor and taste.)

While the pancakes are being panfried to a crispy state, slice the mushrooms and sauté them with a butter and oil combination.

Once the pancakes are ready, place them on a large platter and spread a solid bed (approximately ½ tablespoon) of sour cream over each one. Scatter the mushrooms on top and garnish with cilantro or parsley and, if desired, thin slices of red onion, raw or cooked.

8

Shaggy Mane or Shaggy Ink Cap

Coprinus comatus

MAY TO OCTOBER

Some years ago in Ithaca, the New York State parks department built a new marina, a picnic ground, and a boat launch at the southern tip of Cayuga Lake. Between these new sites, they created large fields with graded topsoil, which was then seeded and covered with a thick layer of composted sludge. Next spring, the grass germinated nicely, and in midsummer, after a cool and rainy week, finally the sun emerged.

My dog Piglet demanded a thorough airing out! We headed out to the freshly established green acres, and as a part-time terrier, Piglet ran in all directions at once, as she was apt to do when released. I followed her erratic running and leaping toward a stand of cottonwood trees and . . . there they were!

I spotted a large family of shaggy manes growing in a long and graceful

*Freshly picked
shaggy manes*

A young shaggy mane in nature

arc. The lineup included all stages and ages of the *Coprinus*... the over-the-hill, shriveled-up dark umbrellas, dripping black ink (which, centuries earlier, monks dipped their goose quills into) and teeter-tottering on a tall, thin leg. There were also middle-aged specimens, still firm and white, showing off their flapper-like layers of serrated skirts. Most adorable, however, were the egg-shaped young, with their tight caps still snugly sitting over the stem. These infants, cut in half, lightly salted, brushed with oil, and quickly broiled, render a fine appetizer. They can also look quite party worthy, decorated with paprika and minced chives, and edged with a necklace of black olives.

The first undulating line of shaggies was just a lure to reveal an even longer procession along the edge of the cottonwoods. Piglet and I rushed back to the car for containers of any kind. This turned out to be the largest haul ever! Even the indefatigable doggy was exhausted after accompanying me back and forth endless times, with yet another box, bag, or shirt full of shaggy manes. Seasoned veteran that she was of my uncontrollable gatherings and foragings, she found this outing dull. The open expanses of landscape with short new grass permitted her prey a full view of what was about to pounce on them. Another disappointment for her was that the aroma of the sludge had expired—there was nothing to roll in!

A young shaggy mane and a mature, inky one, as illustrated in Julius Vincenz von Krombholz's treatise on mushrooms (published 1831–46)

I drove back to our house and unloaded everything into the coolest corner of the masonry basement. I placed the shaggy manes on a long, enamel-topped table and covered them with cold, wet towels, for these mushrooms age quickly. Piglet laid down on her bed sulking, and I also took a short rest and then started to deal with my mountains of gatherings.

The shaggy mane is underestimated by many aficionados due to its delicate perishability (not unlike the 1930s actress Jean Harlow, who also dressed in shaggy-mane dancing garb, and left us when still young). They must be used quickly after picking, because they age rapidly and start to turn dark around the edge of the gills and then upward. The stems tend to be stiff and are best served either pureed or finely minced in soups, sauces, or pâtés.

The young fingerlings, however, hold up very well. I cut them in half, grill the outside, and then fill the small white boat shape with a puree of fried shrimp and garlic or a paste made of boneless and skinless sardines with some of the oil removed and some lemon juice and mayonnaise added. They are tasty warm or cold! If you prefer them warm, put them back in the oven at 350 degrees for ten to fifteen minutes after filling.

For vegetarians, shaggs can also play a welcome role! Fry them golden brown, dice them, and mix them with spears of asparagus cut in half-inch slices; raw red onion, chopped; lots of mixed herbs; and a homemade garlic vinaigrette for the dressing.

Shaggy Manes Gratin

Serves 4 to 6

- 3 medium-size Yukon gold potatoes
- 3 teaspoons salt
- 1 pound young shaggy manes
- 2 to 3 tablespoons butter
- 2 cups béchamel sauce
- ½ cup Parmesan cheese, grated
- 1 tablespoon fresh parsley, minced

Boil the potatoes with 3 teaspoons of salt for approximately 15 minutes. They should still be firm. Peel and slice them.

While the potatoes are boiling, clean the stems of the shaggy manes. These mushrooms generally have very clean caps. Use only the younger ones that have not yet started to darken.

Gently sauté the whole mushrooms in butter on a low flame, until soft but not mushy.

Make a béchamel sauce, approximately 2 cups, and add the shaggy manes to it.

Layer the potatoes in a well-oiled baking dish and then add the mushrooms in the béchamel sauce on top and sprinkle them with freshly grated Parmesan cheese.

Bake covered in a preheated oven, 350°F, for approximately 20 minutes.

Remove the cover and brown under the broiler. Serve with freshly minced parsley.

OUTINGS

✳

Thursday, Fourth of July

Alas, they are up and sassy and everywhere! All my special spots are dotted with deep yellow chanterelles. The forest floor is so generously endowed that all I have to do is sit in the wet and muddy ground and start gathering. Today I brought my Opinel mushroom knife with a five-inch blade and the added features of a cleaning brush and (as only the clever French would provide) a recessed corkscrew, in case one chooses to celebrate early, perhaps with a chilled Vouvray!

I run the sharp blade under the mushroom clusters and pull up handful after handful of golden wealth, bigger and smaller ones together, leaving only the babies for maturing. The chanterelles, so content with the abundant rainfall, have sprung up in places I have never seen them grow before, like the sandy, unstable banks of drainage ditches. I reprimand them for making such a public display of themselves. What a phenomenal year this is for us 'shrooming crazies.

My red and tan Italian willow basket is filled in no time, full to the rim and mounded higher yet. This basket, now thirty years old, is my favorite; it holds about ten pounds of mushrooms. I bought it in Chianti, and today I wish I had negotiated for a larger one. The remainder of the catch is simply placed on a blanket resting on the passenger's seat, also stacked high.

Sated with chanterelles (if there is such a thing), I slowly drive uphill and park under an ancient oak. This accessible expanse of mixed trees, oaks, pines, and maples, almost always offers an array of both edible and poisonous species.

Friday, July 12

Seven a.m., hunting again in the freshly drenched forest. My woods smell even worse this morning. Overripe, waterlogged mushrooms are collapsing into wet ditches. The enormous *Tylopilus felleus* now lie festering in heaps, unified in a light gray mold, hard to decipher cap from stem.

Even though I ventured out primarily to collect the chanterelles, it's the Caesar mushroom that overwhelms me with its exceptional abundance. They display such a brilliant color both cap and stem, and next to and all around them sit the white *ovolini*. At this young stage, when cut in half, the oval sphere looks exactly like a hard-boiled hen offering. The Caesars stand in handsome groupings, one or two tall ones with clusters of small ones at their base, and tennis ball–sized infants randomly popping up in casual circles. I gently place the large ones on a mattress of paper towels at the base of the basket, as they are very brittle. The *ovolini*, which hold up very well, go in a heavy paper shopping bag. The chanterelles are also present in great abundance. Most of them are in pristine condition, revealing sound, hard stems with no infestations.

The mosquitoes are all awake in vast hordes and relentless in their pursuit of my blood. They are stinging my neck and ears, right through a thick glazing of Vicks VapoRub. After some rummaging, I find an old plastic bag under the trunk seat and make myself a shower cap–like headpiece by tying small knots in the corners of the pink-colored bag. In addition to defining the ears, I cut out two holes to see through and a vent for breathing. I catch a glimpse of myself in the window of Hank Jr. and pray there are no hunters aiming at me, for the reflection on the glass reveals a greasy, glowing, pink-headed monster, sporting pointed triangular ears. Even the mosquitoes are perplexed, and their attacks on my head lessen.

Now, back into the thicket for some chanterelles, which are everywhere! They vary in size from five-inch caps to quarter-inch round buttons. They grow in large, friendly families or completely aloof and solo. I leave the little ones; there are already six jars of pickled baby chanterelles in the Frigidaire, along with all the other wild mushroom concoctions, such as butters, pâtés, salads, and soups.

In about forty-five minutes, two baskets, a paper bag, and an aluminum pie plate are filled with orange and yellow. The colors sparkle against the black-ribbed bed liner. This is truly a fabulous 'shrooming summer, the best in thirty years!

Back to the woods! I am exhausted from my last outing, just a day ago, but one has to do what has to be done, especially when obsessed, like I am.

The roadside colors are now completely dominated by vibrant orange daylilies. They border the fields, where the plow has allotted them a few feet to thrive between the crops and the drainage ditches. An occasional straggly wild pea also competes to display multiple small blossoms of purple and pale pink. I revisit all my spots that I didn't get to yesterday, and again, in less than an hour, two baskets are mounded tall with gold chanterelles.

It is already very hot and humid, and the insects are relentless. I keep re-basting my face, neck, and hands in Vicks VapoRub and push my welding glasses tight over my eyes. The bitter mushrooms, *Tylopilus felleus*, have matured to the size of saddles, their huge dark caps are turning gray and moldy, and the stench of decay has permeated the hot air. I lift a few flat stones and place them in back of the truck (to use in my herb garden to contain weeds), cut a large bouquet of lilies, and am ready to head back home, when the temptation to peruse one more location overwhelms me. I obey my instincts. Entering a narrow clearing between two large oaks close to the road, I remain calm and optimistic. To the right, cheerfully draining, is a large concrete culvert, much replenished with yesterday's heavy rains.

And then I glance in back of the oaks, toward a small mossy plateau which has erupted in the thin, tall, and dark shapes of the black trumpet, the *Craterellus cornucopioides*, one of my most favorite species! One basket of chanterelles gets evicted onto a blanket on the passenger's side, and sitting amidst the young trumpets, I carefully lift them out, snip off their root, and refill the basket.

By now, many russulas have made their debut, sporting deep red, green, charcoal, pink, and pale yellow caps. I still have not forgiven them for giving me an unexpected, unpleasant druggy high fifty years ago. At the farm in Dover, Massachusetts, belonging to the family of Constance Saltonstall, my partner at the time, I had sautéed some pink and red russulas and served them at dinner that night. Connie's grandfather, Senator Leverett Saltonstall, as well as his wife declined my offer, as did other dinner guests; only Connie and I sampled a small portion. She was fine, but I woke up in the middle of the night feeling disoriented and somewhat dizzy. By morning, things were back to normal, and this was my one and only unpleasant incident with wild mushroom consumption. In Germany, I used to consume vast quantities of this species, but in the U.S.A. some of the red-colored specimens harbor psychedelic properties. After half a century, I should forgive and forget; many russulas are highly edible and quite tasty. But today is not the right time, because I am preoccupied with the easygoing, friendly ones, chanterelles—one color fits all!

As I walk back to the truck, I spot an astonishing display . . . on a bright green mossy hillock sits a single, almost twenty-inch-tall *Amanita caesarea*. Ave Caesar! The bright orange glistening crown, resting on its elegant, deep yellow pedestal stem, is utterly majestic. Reminds me of a personal honor guard of some long-forgotten Persian queen.

Sunday, July 14
(Bastille Day)

The weather forecast is predicting several days of ninety-degree heat, so I am in the woods early, at 6:30. The eastern sun was rising slowly as I drove through one of the small villages leading to my woods. The usual upstate New York fare: a one-story, cement-block volunteer fire station, a hillock cemetery with indecisively leaning old gravestones, a long-abandoned mom-and-pop store closed up with chipboard, a former Greek revival home clad in asphalt shingles, half painted strawberry pink, and for the more upscale residents, a grouping of vinyl-sided double-wides under three mostly dead maples. A full array of speed limits were posted in this hamlet, rising from 20 to 35 m.p.h. and then, for a speedy exit south, a flowing 40 m.p.h.

The sunlight focused on the front facade of a formerly white wooden church with an ornate steeple still firmly resting on the roof, but broken windows, a sagging entrance door, and weeds growing through the front steps kept the golden rays from any success at elation or elevation. Not far in back of the old church, I could see the new one, obscured by a cornfield, with a steeple the size of a toothpick. How will this ill-built edifice help us play the cello on cloud nine?

O n the road again, escorted by flocks of crows. Lots of pre-pounded meat filets on the asphalt surface, left by twitched-out drivers revving their automobiles to escape the ninety-six-degree heat. Today I arrive in the 'shrooming lo-cale at 6:30 a.m., because the forecast is predicting beastly heat and stulti-fying humidity. I am already stupefied, hearing these predictions. Having learned my lesson three days ago (when I got riddled with insect bites), I park the truck under some large shady oaks and lather myself in my fa-vorite mentholated rub, put on a long-sleeved shirt, knee socks, long cot-ton work pants, all-terrain sneakers, a visored Red Sox cap, and lastly a pair of welding glasses. All right, mosquitoes, black flies, deer ticks, stink bugs, wasps, spiders, and other destined inheritors of this planet, try to molest me! From the back of the truck I lift out my basket, bamboo walk-ing stick, and ever-capable Opinel knife.

This early morning I'm in pursuit of the trompette de la mort, which I left to mature a few days ago. This heavenly mushroom clan had sent up numerous tall, elegant trumpets, which now had burst into raggedy gray-ish black clumps. The trumpet is very easy to pick, for its contact with the soil is quite delicate, a thin, long stem that barely penetrates the surface it rises from. The aroma rising from a pan full of simmering trumpets is the closest we can get to the grandeur of the mostly European black truffle, the cost of which is escalating yearly.

The putrid odor of decaying 'shrooms is very pronounced this morn-ing, even more than on my last outing, but even though so much is shriv-eling up or keeling over from rot, small healthy mushrooms are emerging in their place. It is my job to bring them home before the hundred-degree heat leads them to an early demise.

Summer riches: chanterelles, Caesars, boletes, and black trumpets

9

Oyster Mushroom

Pleurotus ostreatus

JULY TO SEPTEMBER

The *Pleurotus ostreatus* is a clustered shelf-like growth that lives off its host, usually a sickly maple, but occasionally an aspen, birch, or oak. Sometimes it will conveniently nestle four to five feet up on the tree, or it will squat at the base, but every so often it can also thrive way up near the crown. What to do with a lovely cluster fifteen to twenty feet high? Do you contemplate philosophically, like the fox, that it is probably not that tasty? Of course not. Procure a long branch with a fork at the end and coax the morsels down. Often I stand on the roof of my truck cab to facilitate the desired result. Sometimes the only way is to climb the tree, which can result in unintended consequences, especially since oysters prefer mature trees in sickly health.

For lazier oyster gatherers, there is always the horizontal opportunity, i.e., the felled tree, left to decay, infused with oyster mycellum that sprouts in bountiful families. The oceanic nomen for this delicacy refers not only to its shape but also to its flavor. When cooked gently, the oyster actually evokes a lovely fresh seafood flavor. The equally prized *Laetiporus sulphureus*, or sulfur shelf (see chapter 10), has this quality as well.

Professor H. Peter Kahn, already introduced in the meadow mushroom

Freshly picked oyster mushrooms

Oyster mushrooms in nature

chapter and for many years by then Peter to me, chose to participate in this chapter also. At that time, in the late 1960s, I lived in an enormous hay barn, AD 1883, in Newfield, New York. My partner then, Constance Saltonstall, and I had bought the agricultural structure sitting on forty-five acres of farmland as well as some steep hillside with mixed trees. I had just returned from a successful oyster hunt when I heard a car door slam. The barn's large rolling doors facing the pond were open, and a few minutes later a disheveled Peter appeared with supermarket shopping bags, three of them, filled with more oyster mushrooms. I compromised and decided to clean and prepare one bag of his catch and one bag from my own outing.

The preparation took no time at all. We both sat down around a large oval table, released the mushrooms from their paper confinements, cut off the short woody stems, and lightly brushed the irregular gills free of insects and bark chips. Peter's oysters had a slightly glossy gray hue, whereas mine were a paler whitish color. As we subdued our catch we talked, as we were both apt to do, about everything under the sun and a few things even under the moon. Hedy Lamarr, my most glamorous hen, sashayed over. She had two black single feathers on top of her head. I offered her some stem trimmings, which she examined carefully before rejecting them. Our pet ducks landed back on the pond; one half had white pom-poms on their heads, while the others were more modest. Then, in the afternoon sun, the rest of the chickens appeared, as well as three dogs and the sole cat. Two horses in the cellar thankfully stayed in their stalls, grinding hay with their ample teeth.

The oysters began to succumb to the hot olive oil, salt, and red pepper, and a deep aroma swirled through the chestnut and cedar barn. The colonel made an entrance; a white male goat, medium size, bearded with square pupils. Colonel "Ghèbètté" named himself, for that was the sound he would make. He got us out of many financial crises by eating the bills that had accumulated in the corner pockets of our pool table. All of our pets were hand-me-downs, formerly destitute, now living in grand style.

The dinner was ready. I stirred in some fresh baby spinach just before serving the simmered oysters, which were accompanied with well-chilled Alsatian gewürztraminer and Connie's homemade biscuits. Only gurgles and grunts of appreciation were heard. Unlike me, Peter told me exactly where he had found his bounty, and just like me, I never told anyone where I had found mine.

Oyster Mushrooms over Cod or Haddock

Serves 4

—◦—

- ½ to ¾ pound oyster mushrooms
- 1 large clove of garlic, minced
- 1 medium-size onion, finely chopped
- 2 teaspoons lemon zest
- 1 tablespoon fresh parsley
- 1 tablespoon fresh basil or chives
- 4 fresh fillets of cod or haddock (about 1½ pounds)
- 2 to 3 tablespoons butter
- Salt
- Radicchio
- Fresh parsley
- 2 lemons

Go along with their name and serve oyster mushrooms with seafood. They will work in perfect harmony!

Destem the mushrooms and panfry the caps with minced garlic, finely chopped onion, a touch of lemon zest, and the herbs.

Sauté the fish fillets in butter and salt to a light brown on both sides. Place in a deep dish on a bed of radicchio, and ladle the sautéed mushrooms over them.

Cut the lemons in quarter wedges for use and place them around the edge of the platter in a decorative fashion, along with sprigs of parsley. Serve with a crisp, dry white wine and thinly sliced bread.

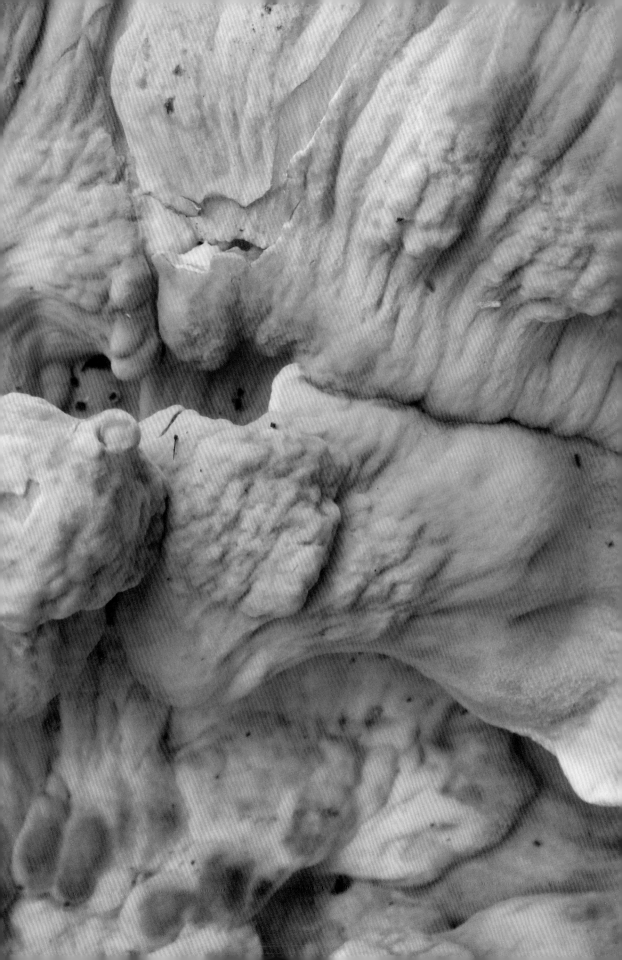

10

Chicken Mushroom or Sulfur Shelf

Laetiporus sulphureus

MAY TO NOVEMBER

The *Laetiporus sulphureus*, along with the *Grifola frondosa*, a.k.a. hen of the woods or maitake, is a "parasitic" fruit, hanging off the declining wood of an oak, a maple, or occasionally a willow. This is one of the largest bracket fungi in the forest. It can emerge in a myriad of clusters on the bark or in the branch crotches of an affected tree, or it can appear as a single, sometimes gigantic mass of golden orange protrusions resting on a stump it favors.

A friend of mine and fledgling mushroom aficionado spotted a colossal cluster on the agricultural quad of Cornell University. The beast barely fit into the trunk of a sedan and, after minimal cleaning, rendered edible parts close to forty pounds. This delightful *sulphureus* was also in the bloom of youth; all parts were soft and succulent, even the centers and modest root sections. This is the ideal mushroom for inexperienced hunters, for nothing else looks like it, and the rewards of finding a large young specimen are simply delicious.

Close-up of a chicken mushroom

Chicken mushrooms on a tree

The bright yellow undersides (bracket bellies) of the lobes and the brilliant orange upper shelves are startling in a deep dark forest, like some exotic escapee from a Caribbean rainforest. In October, with so much of nature subdued and ready for a long sleep, here comes the *sulphureus* ready to tango. Well, long live brazen varieties and their courage to be bold and different!

My own monumental haul occurred in late fall on Mason's Island, offshore from New Haven, Connecticut. Sarah and I were on our way, in the pouring rain, to procure something edible from a mainland supermarket. Lo and behold, after several bridges, where the road took a steep turn west to the coast, our headlights revealed what I took to be a discarded brightly colored rain slicker, but as I completed the turn, I could decipher a large log and atop it no rain slicker at all . . . instead several closely staked, superb specimens of the *sulphureus*, perched obediently. Our island hosts, former classmates from the Rhode Island School of Design, were surprised when we returned quite quickly with three pounds of fettuccini, heavy cream, a greenhouse bouquet of basil, and a bottle of white vermouth. I refused to comment on the large, mysterious bundle wrapped in my raincoat. I requested their indulgence in our secretive ways and promised a most memorable supper, especially if they left us be in the kitchen for forty-five minutes or so. In the allotted time we boiled the pasta al dente, spread it on a large, warmed platter, and then ladled the pièce de résistance on it: thin-sliced *sulphureus* sautéed in olive oil with roasted tomatoes, garlic, salt, and pepper, and then revitalized with white vermouth, fresh cream, and shredded basil.

My dinner guests marveled at the flavors and began to guess various ingredients. Veal was suggested, as well as Cornish game hen or perhaps Thai eggplant. No one guessed wild mushrooms, but after dinner the plates, pots, pans, and platter got polished with remaining pieces of bread amid hums of deep satisfaction.

Some mushroom gatherers claim sulfur shelf tastes like chicken, as its other names, "chicken mushroom" and "chicken of the woods," might suggest. Personally I think its delicate flavor is more lobster- or crab-like. But the name "lobster mushroom" has been given to another species, *Hypomyces lactifluorum*, a parasitic growth that absconds with its host mushrooms. It is also bright orange in the wild. I shy away from this absorber, for I have no guarantee that it has not consumed either a poisonous *Russula* or a bitter *Lactarius*. Since lobster mushrooms are now sold commercially, one could assume they have eliminated these concerns.

Chicken mushrooms on a fallen log

Sulfur Shelf Pizza

Serves 4

- Twelve-inch pizza dough
- ½ cup tomato sauce seasoned with herbs and garlic
- 1 ball coarsely grated mozzarella
- ½ pound sulfur shelf or hen of the woods*
- 1 small onion
- ½ cup grated Parmesan
- Basil pesto (optional)

* Use only the soft tips of the mushrooms. The harder sections can be saved for a broth.

Preheat oven to 400°F. Heat pizza stone. Stretch the pizza dough and apply the prepared tomato sauce and mozzarella.

Panfry the mushrooms with onions until both are soft and cooked through, approximately 15 minutes.

Scatter the mushrooms over the pizza. Apply dollops of pesto, if desired, and top with Parmesan.

Bake in oven for 10 minutes or until the cheese is bubbly and crust is light brown.

11

Giant Puffball & Warted Puffball

Calvatia gigantea & Lycoperdon perlatum

JULY TO OCTOBER

The giant puffball, a white ball (sometimes elongated) that actually varies widely in size, may be found solo or in a family setting. It grows where it wants to be, near manure piles, in backyards, on lawns and golf courses, in meadows and mulched beds, but also where you would not expect it to be, under pines, in dumps, or in flower gardens. (I do not like picking mushrooms on golf courses; the amount of fertilizers and pesticides used is worrisome.) The puffball appears mid- to late summer and, due to its size, is one of the easiest to find and safest to eat, because it has no evil relatives. The outer skin resembles thin felt and should be removed prior to cooking.

I pick puffballs "safari style," sitting propped high on pillows in Hank

The author with two
giant puffballs

A giant puffball in nature

Jr., my Ford Ranger pickup with a deep blue body and bright silver accessories, a great 'shrooming companion.

The warted, or gem-studded, puffball is the smallest cousin of the giant puffball, and I consider it very tasty indeed. The outside of the *perlatum* is covered with minute white granules, and the skin under it is more tender than that of its big cousin. So, all that is needed for preparation is to trim off its stubby root and brush any sand or soil from its belly. Then, depending on its size, cut the body into halves or quarters and proceed to cook.

The largest and tastiest batch of *perlatum* Sarah and I procured together was on the Isle of Wight, in the English Channel. I had received a Winston Churchill Travelling Fellowship, awarded by the English-Speaking Union, to study, draw and photograph nineteenth- and twentieth-century storefronts. The evaluation of British fungi was certainly not included in the award. A couple, both architects and good friends of Sarah's, invited

Giant puffballs of various sizes

us for a few days of nautical adventures aboard their trimaran, which was rather miniature for four people. Wight is a large isle (148 square miles) with fossil-rich shores, fine vacation cottages, and fluffy red squirrels. Charles Dickens, Jeremy Irons, and David Niven all resided on the island, but its most important former resident was Queen Victoria, who built her enormous summer home, Osborne House, there. The isle provides a warmer microclimate that beckoned the perpetually older monarch.

We docked not far from the town of Cowes and decided to explore the craggy and rough coastline . . . and there they were! Dainty white *Lycoperdon perlatum*, nestled in scrubby grass, as far as the eye could see. Gathering commenced. We collected them in shirts and sweaters and cones of rolled-up newspaper.

That evening, in the boat's bowels, in a galley about two by two feet, with a single gas burner, I boiled Italian fettuccini for four, transferred

Giant puffballs sliced, peeled, and cubed

the pasta into a clean-scrubbed basin, and in the same pot (also the only one) lightly browned onions and garlic in butter, added a large mound of the freshly picked 'shrooms, halved, and continued sautéing until everything was a deep golden color. White wine was added, followed by a pint of English heavy cream. There was almost no fighting or biting among the ingredients; all looked homogeneous. The grand finale was a topping of finely minced wild mint and leeks, also gathered ashore. Two architects and two preservationists ate splendidly, and toasted, with Victoria Regina's majestic residence looming in the background.

Of all European countries, England remains the most mycophobic. Even the great culinary persuader, Elizabeth David, was unable to convince the Brits otherwise, although getting them not to boil vegetables for endless hours was one of her crowning achievements. Calling

Warted puffballs in nature

the magnificent *Boletus edulis* a "penny bun" is indicative of the British attitude. . . . I could understand a ten-pound roll, but hardly such small change.

I don't recall finding mushrooms in Scotland or Ireland, but commercially grown *Agaricus* buttons, pickled, are starting to appear at plowman's lunches served in brewpubs.

Baked Puffball

Serves 4 to 6

⚬ 1 medium-size puffball
⚬ 2 large eggs
⚬ Salt
⚬ Fine ground white pepper
⚬ Breadcrumbs or panko seasoned with Italian herbs
⚬ Olive oil
⚬ ½ cup mayonnaise
⚬ ½ cup salsa picante
⚬ Cilantro, finely minced
⚬ 1 ripe tomato, if desired

Peel off the puffball's outer skin, which is quite tough, and dice the sphere into roughly 2 by 2 inch squares about 1 inch thick. (Due to the mushroom's roundness, you may end up with a few small slices that are hard to convert to a square shape, but you can save these to use in a different dish.)

Beat the eggs and add salt and pepper. Pour the egg batter into a shallow pan and add the mushroom squares. Turn the squares occasionally with a flat wooden spoon, so that all edges absorb the batter evenly. Let the ingredients sit at room temperature for an hour.

On a sizable cutting board or counter, spread the breadcrumbs or panko in a thick, even layer. By hand or with tongs, cover all edges of the puffball squares with an even coating of crumbs.

Place the squares onto an olive oil–primed baking platter and bake in a preheated oven at 350°F for 10 to 15 minutes. Set the oven to broil and turn over all the squares to achieve a crisp golden brown top and bottom.

Make a Spanish-style dipping sauce to serve with the puffball squares: mix the mayonnaise with the salsa picante, top with finely minced cilantro, and, if desired, encircle with some tomato wedges for a decorative effect.

Perlatum over Squash

Serves 4

- 1 fall squash such as delicata or acorn
- 2 tablespoons butter
- 1 medium-size onion, minced
- 1 large clove of garlic, chopped
- 1 cup diced tomatoes (fresh or canned)
- ½ to ¾ pound *perlatum*
- Green onions

Lightly brush any dirt from the mushrooms. They usually grow in hygienic settings such as grass or pine needles. Slice large ones in half and leave small ones whole.

Bake the squash.

Make a tomato sauce: Lightly panfry the minced onions and chopped garlic in butter, and add the tomatoes. Simmer together for 10 to 15 minutes.

Panfry the mushrooms in butter until they are light brown.

Mash the squash and layer it on the plate. Add the tomato sauce, just enough to taste. Top with *perlatum* and green onions.

12

Parasol Mushroom

Macrolepiota procera

AUGUST TO OCTOBER

& Shaggy Parasol Mushroom

Chlorophyllum rhacodes

JUNE TO OCTOBER

I have found *Macrolepiota procera*, the "lady's parasol," with a cap up to twelve inches wide. It is the largest member of the family Agaricaceae. These mushrooms enjoy rich soil and even more nutritious compost piles, but they can also thrive in organic fields and meadows. The large, shaggy caps rest on long stems circled by a casual white ring. (The stems are stringy and often tough, and best used in broths or pureed in pâtés.)

The author with a large parasol mushroom

Young shaggy parasols in nature

A parasol mushroom in nature

When young, parasols emerge ball-shaped, and as they mature, they lift dramatically upward on their long, thin stems, and then the caps flatten and widen. At first they display white gills, which later turn to a light beige. This species is very seldom inundated with invasive insects or slugs.

Their first cousin, which looks very much alike, is called the *Chlorophyllum rhacodes* or shaggy parasol. It is considerably more scaly, with flakes all over its cap. It is also edible and tasty! Both species of parasol are very dependable mushrooms, capable of repeated arrivals, not just one single fruiting, in the same size and location year after year.

Parasols' large, circular caps open doors to imaginative culinary directions. They hold their shape well and are delicious broiled with vegetables, fish, or sausage. Younger and smaller specimens lend themselves to stuffed-cap recipes. Another suggestion for serving parasols: cut them into attractive sections or pieces, batter in cream and eggs, deep-fry in olive oil, and serve with thin-sliced vegetables such as carrots and zucchini, decorated with fresh herbs.

Due to its size, elegant proportions, and umbrella-sized cap, the parasol is always rewarding to hunt. When I make a good haul, I spread a tarp in back of my pickup, Hank Jr. Then I lay the caps gills down and rush my collection home to commence preparations. Somewhat later phone calls are made, invitations are accepted, and the parasols emerge, roasted and bubbling with delicious fillings. Such an evening procures reciprocal invitations from friends and gourmands who create dishes with garlic scapes, nettles, forest nuts, and other seasonal delicacies.

A harvest of shaggy parasols at various stages of growth

Stuffed Parasol Caps

Serves 3

- 6 large parasol mushrooms
- Olive oil
- 2 large garlic cloves, finely chopped
- 2 small onions, minced
- 2 small celery stalks, finely chopped
- 2 cups breadcrumbs
- 1 cup grated Parmigiano Reggiano
- Salt and pepper
- If desired, 1 pound pan-fried Italian sausage, with excess fat drained off

The parasol mushroom has a delicious flavor, more distinctive than some of its cousins in the agaricus family.

Brush off any residual dirt from the caps and stems. Carefully remove the stems where they join the cap. Place the caps gill side up in a hot frying pan with 2 tablespoons of olive oil. Gently brown for 3 to 4 minutes. Remove from pan and cool.

Make the stuffing: Chop the stems and combine them with the garlic, onion, celery, breadcrumbs, and Parmigiano Reggiano, with salt and pepper to taste. If desired, add cooked Italian sausage. The quantity of the stuffing ingredients can be adjusted based on the size of the caps and the cook's preference for flavor.

After the stuffing is thoroughly mixed, mound it on the gill side of the caps. Drizzle the stuffed caps generously with olive oil and sprinkle with more grated Parmesan cheese before placing them under a preheated broiler. Keep a close eye on them, since they won't take more than 5 to 7 minutes to cook. They can be served on a bed of cooked greens such as spinach or kale.

OUTINGS

❋

Late Summer

W hat a year! Divine excess! My regimen of twice-a-week outings, and occasionally a Saturday or Sunday, has been immensely rewarding. Our newly purchased upright freezer is packed to the brim with quick-blanched chanterelles, oysters, black trumpets, and even a round of *Hydnum albidum*, unusual for the tiny toothlike tentacles affixed to the underside of its cap. A fine mushroom that I seldom find in large numbers.

Now that August has arrived with less rain, I have slowed down a little, which is good, for I have also filled my friends' freezers, leaving hasty notes claiming the 'shroom occupancy is strictly temporary. These comments turned out to be untrue. The freezer we bought, secondhand at a neighbor's yard sale, purred and hummed for twenty-four hours and then expired with a whine. More hurried stashing away here and there, additional pushing and stacking in the overcrowded Frigidaire, and finally a trip into the city of Ithaca to procure a new freezer chest.

I commence some energetic trading as well. A 'shroom pâté, made with slippery jacks and oyster mushrooms, fetches a fine bottle of locally made Riesling, black trumpet butter (a small dish) is exchanged for a bag of freshly roasted coffee, and half a pound of fresh chanterelles return as two pints of farm-picked blueberries. The trades are not negotiated, but they are never disappointing. Yesterday, a platter of pickled baby chanterelles dressed in fresh herbs and good olive oil procured a large jar of sheep-milk yogurt, Greek style. If only small, regional farming had started up in America after World War II, we would have been spared the odious strip-mall megamarkets selling everything, and therefore nothing! All the trade items just mentioned are grown, harvested, or manufactured right here in Trumansburg or nearby; only the coffee beans are world travelers, and with global warming upon us, that too could change.

August 23

Roadsides have been overtaken by scruffy, bright blue phlox. The milkweed is still standing firm, and cheerful buttercups seem happy to hang with everything else. Large tracts of soybeans have curious invaders. Single cornstalks, tall and tasseled, have shot upward randomly, above the meeker soybean plane, probably stragglers from last summer's crop. Much of the hay has already been cut and, after the ordeal, is now resting in enormous rolled wheels sheathed in transparent plastic. How much nicer looking these bales are than the long rolls of hay wrapped in opaque white sheets, resembling beached albino whales.

Fall

A noontime hunt today, under an indecisive sky, both blue and gray. The sturdy thistle plants have turned into skeletons, sloppily shedding silver hairs; the stands of maples are succumbing to September shades. Only the sumacs look young and healthy.

The other bumper crop this year is apples. The overburdened branches slope down steeply, the unhumble ones break. Big piles of fruit are resting under their crowns. No one seems to be making applesauce or pie or cider . . . the time-consuming activities of the past are relegated to cider mills and fruit stands.

Stems and Pieces

My major outings are not just about gathering 'shrooms. I do love to be in a forest at sunup, the light in which we all thrive. The paths I choose to walk or drive on are often old lumber trails, narrow, rutted, overgrown. Aggressive hawks dive-bomb above me; they use the open space higher up to spread their wings and spot their prey. Early songbirds are already chirping, train-whistling, warning, cooing. A little later the woodpeckers commence with their precise tapping, banging, and drumming, mostly succeeding in obtaining breakfast. I spot lots of deer. Pregnant does in early summer, with playful twins in late fall. I only occasionally spot a buck, but in Maine I was observed by a monumental bull moose proudly balancing a candelabra on his head. Sometimes, exhausted, I sit on some moss, and wait, and let worldly concerns drift out of my head.

At first, it seems to be quiet, even still, but it is not. Tiny, gentle sounds emerge, buzzing, humming, fluttering—bees, butterflies, mosquitoes, ants, snails, everyone preoccupied with accomplishing their daily tasks. Occasionally a small snake will slither by, or a turtle will waddle toward a stream, or a beaver will start carving around a chosen tree. They all seem oblivious of my presence, as it should be. On a bright, sunny day, I stop looking for mushrooms around noontime; the whole forest floor gets dappled with bright sunspots, and I no longer run toward golden patches assuming them to be large stands of chanterelles. Still, they are beautiful illusions.

One morning I entered the woods really early, just before dawn. Leaving a more open area, I advanced toward a denser, darker wall of trees. Just then the sun emerged in back of me, and I moved more quickly. At first I could not grasp what was becoming visible just ahead. What I was staring at was a continuous weave of cobwebs, spanning from tree to branch to leaf. Each interlaced edge glowed with thousands of jewel-like pendants, as the rising sun ignited each tiny pearl of dew. I fell on my knees, overwhelmed by this visual spectacle. The only other time in my life I have been so moved was watching the Ganesh Himal mountain range in Nepal burned by the rising sun, with every craggy protuberance, ledge, and fold baking in deep, fiery golden pinks and reds … a breathtaking display, soul and body warming, especially after I spent the night shivering in a cotton suit lined with yak wool (purchased in a Kathmandu market). Overnight lodgings were cots in a plank shed, shabbily assembled at a base camp, with thin, raggedy cotton blankets and a night temperature hovering at twenty degrees.

Even the famed theater and opera curtains going up in Paris, London, Prague, Saint Petersburg, Vienna, or Berlin, which I was privileged to see and hear, could not begin to rival these natural mirages.

There are also sad and depressing aspects of returning to beloved forests year after year. To have to witness the disrespect so many people have for the environment that facilitates their very existence. The natural environment, our common and shared living room, abused by dumping, polluting, littering.

The author with puffballs, an autumn mushroom

I think that I shall never see
A billboard lovely as a tree.
Indeed, unless the billboards fall
I'll never see a tree at all.
      —Ogden Nash, "Song of the Open Road"

Wild Mushroom Pâté

Serves 4 to 6

⁕⟡⁕

- 1½ pounds larger mushrooms (slippery jacks, chanterelles, *Agaricus*, honey mushrooms, etc.)
- 8 ounces cream cheese
- 1½ sticks butter
- 3 eggs
- Salt
- White pepper
- Dried herbs (basil, oregano, parsley, etc.)
- Olive oil

Clean and chop the mushrooms and lay them on a kitchen towel or paper napkins to absorb some of the moisture from cleaning. Transfer the chopped mushrooms into a Cuisinart or blender and mix them until smooth and creamy. If you own a small blender, this process might require two or three separate spins. Add the cream cheese (cut up into smaller pieces), butter (melted), raw eggs, salt, pepper, and dried herbs. Reblend the entire mixture.

Grease small Teflon baking pans (about 6 inches long, 3 inches wide, and 2 inches tall) with olive oil. Spoon the mixture into the small pans about a quarter inch down from the top rim. Preheat the oven to 360°F. Set the small pans into a large baking pan filled with about 1 inch of water. Bake about 50 minutes. Turn the heat up to 400°F for the last 10 minutes, and the pâté-to-be will rise right to the top of the small pan.

Take the pâté out of the tray and pierce it with a long wooden toothpick to make sure it is fully and completely baked. Once it is at room temperature, put it into the refrigerator and let it "set up."

Serve either cold or at room temperature on crackers or thin-sliced white bread.

The author studying the book of nature at La Foce, Val d'Orcia, Italy

RECOMMENDED
READING

Bessette, Alan E., and Arleen R. Bessette. *Common Edible and Poisonous Mushrooms of New York.* Syracuse, NY: Syracuse University Press, 2006.

Carluccio, Antonio. *A Passion for Mushrooms.* Topsfield, MA: Salem House, 1989.

Czernecki, Jack. *A Cook's Book of Mushrooms: With 100 Recipes for Common and Uncommon Varieties.* New York: Artisan, 1995.

Hudler, George W. *Magical Mushrooms, Mischievous Molds.* Princeton, NJ: Princeton University Press, 1998.

Jordan, Peter, and Steven Wheeler. *The Practical Mushroom Encyclopedia: Identifying, Picking and Cooking with Mushrooms.* London: Southwater, 2000.

Kleijn, H. *Mushrooms and Other Fungi: Their Form and Colour.* Garden City, NY: Doubleday, 1962.

Marley, Greg A. *Mushrooms for Health: Medicinal Secrets of Northeastern Fungi.* Rockport, ME: Down East Books, 2009.

Pilát, Albert, and Otto Ušák. *A Handbook of Mushrooms.* London: Spring Books, 1959.

N.B. The scientific nomenclature for mushrooms is changing rapidly as a result of genetic research, and usages may vary from book to book.

INDEX

Page numbers in *italics* refer to illustrations.

ACKNOWLEDGMENTS

We would like to thank publisher David Fabricant and his team at Abbeville Press for their confidence and patience in bringing this book to publication. We would also like to thank our well-connected friends Elvira Brockman and her sister Rose Viggiano, who made the right contacts with editors Pat Fogerty and Amy Hughes. They too have our deep appreciation for steering this toward Abbeville. And finally we would like to recognize our valued ongoing friendship with Peggy Haine and Eric Goodman, two of the earliest supporters of the Finger Lakes' local food and wine scene, which has had an important influence on recognizing the culinary importance of wild mushrooms.

ABOUT THE AUTHOR & PHOTOGRAPHER

Victoria Romanoff has been collecting mushrooms since her early years in Latvia, before she and her mother fled to Germany to escape the Soviet invasion in 1944. It was knowledge that helped them survive seven years in various Displaced Persons camps in Germany.

Upon arrival in the U.S., Victoria embarked on learning English by going to the movies, instead of school, and taking her cues from Hollywood stars such as Bette Davis. Her artistic abilities gave her a place at Rhode Island School of Design and then a full graduate scholarship in fine arts to Cornell University.

A love of the Finger Lakes region, including its natural settings for mushrooms, was a determining factor in her decision to remain in Tompkins County after college. Victoria and her partner, Sarah Adams, have had a very well-respected and successful preservation, restoration, and design firm, V. Romanoff & Associates, for over forty years.

Sarah has a background in American architecture and history. Photography has been a lifelong interest. Her images have been featured in a number of preservation articles and the publication *New York State Storefronts: Stone through Cararra, Endangered Species in a World of Plastic.*

Foreign travel, often related to grants awarded to study historic architecture, has given them an opportunity to sample and photograph wild mushrooms in many different settings. Italian trattorias inspired them to open the first wood-fired pizza restaurant in Ithaca, Trattoria Tre Stelle, where wild mushrooms were a menu favorite. Preparing and enjoying wild mushrooms with friends is a shared passion.

All photographs herein are by Sarah Adams,
with the exception of the following:
Constance Saltonstall: pp. 6, 117
Eve Cohen: p. 11
Peter H. Raven Library, Missouri Botanical Garden/
Biodiversity Heritage Library: p. 77

"Song of the Open Road" copyright © 1932 Ogden Nash.
Reprinted by permission of Curtis Brown, Ltd.

Editor: David Fabricant
Production editor: Lauren Bucca
Designer: Misha Beletsky
Production manager: Louise Kurtz
Indexer: Peter Rooney

First edition
1 3 5 7 9 10 8 6 4 2

ISBN 978-0-7892-1429-4

Library of Congress Cataloging-in-Publication Data
available upon request

For bulk and premium sales and for text adoption proce-
dures, write to Customer Service Manager, Abbeville Press,
655 Third Avenue, New York, NY 10017, or call
1-800-ARTBOOK (U.S. only).

Visit Abbeville Press online at www.abbeville.com.